혹시 파란색 진돗개 보셨어요?

Have You Seen a Blue Jindo Dog?

1판 1쇄 · 1st edition published	2021. 8. 2
1판 2쇄 · 2nd edition published	2022. 9. 26
지은이 · Written by	장성원 Kanari Jones, TalkToMeInKorean
책임편집 · Edited by	TalkToMeInKorean
디자인 · Designed by	선윤아 Yoona Sun
녹음 · Voice Recordings by	TalkToMeInKorean
펴낸곳 · Published by	롱테일북스 Longtail Books
펴낸이 · Publisher	이수영 Su Young Lee
편집 · Copy-edited by	김보경 Florence Kim
주소 · Address	04033 서울특별시 마포구 양화로 113, 3층(서교동, 순흥빌딩)
	3rd Floor, 113 Yanghwa-ro, Mapo-gu, Seoul, KOREA
이메일 · E-mail	TTMIK@longtailbooks.co.kr
ISBN	979-11-91343-20-5 13710

TTMIK - TALK TO ME IN KOREAN

혹시 파란색 진돗개 보셨어요?

Have You Seen a Blue Jindo Dog?

Created by
Kanari Jones & TalkToMeInKorean

T___T_ M_
I_ K_____

Why We Created This Book

This book was created for everyone who loves good stories and beautiful illustrations, but also with Korean learners in mind. Co-written by the team behind Talk To Me In Korean, the world's leading Korean language education brand, the book cleverly uses vocabulary and sentence structures that beginner and intermediate learners of the Korean language can recognize and learn.

Reading is an important part of language learning, but it is not easy to find the right materials for learners who are not advanced yet. Books written for Korean children are often too short or too advanced for learners, and reading materials for learners can be too academic. With this book, we want to give you both a pleasant reading experience and a good language-learning experience.

Now, before you start reading the book and embark on your journey to find the blue Jindo dog, here are a few things to note:

- ✓ Most sentences in this book use grammar points introduced in levels 1 to 5 in the Talk To Me In Korean Essential Curriculum.

- ✓ In Korean, single quotation marks are used for quoting thoughts in one's head, and double quotation marks are used for spoken words.

- ✓ All the characters in this book feature animals that live in Korea.

Who Co-wrote This Book

장성원 '까나리존스' / Sung-won Jang a.k.a. Kanari Jones

취미는 그림. 고양이 '난로'와 '담요'와 함께 지내고 있습니다. 서울에서 순수미술을 전공했고 현재는 메이커 스페이스 '릴리쿰'에서 놀이 문화에 대한 창작 활동을 하고 있습니다. 판화와 자수에 관심이 많습니다.

Sung-won Jang is an illustrator who spends way too much time taking photos of his cute cats, Stove and Blanket. He majored in fine arts and currently creates recreational and cultural activities. He also loves engraving and embroidery.

instagram @kanarijones

Have You Seen a Blue Jindo Dog?

You can listen to the story read by
a native speaker on our website,
talktomeinkorean.com/audio.

What Characters Are in the Story

삽살 Sapsal
이야기의 주인공 The main character of this story

사라진 친구 진이를 찾고 있다. 착한 마음씨로
누구하고도 잘 어울린다. 귀신을 볼 수 있는 능력이
있는데, 귀신이랑도 친하게 지낸다.

She is looking for her missing friend, Jin. She has a
kind spirit, so she gets along well with anyone. She has
the ability to see ghosts, but she even gets along with
them.

진 Jin
삽살이의 친구 Sapsal's friend

갑자기 말도 없이 사라졌다. 진이는 어디로 갔을까?

He disappeared all of a sudden without a word.
Where do you think Jin has gone?

책오리 The Book-Duck
어느 날 갑자기 나타난 신기한 오리 An interesting duck
who suddenly appeared one day

알 수 없는 이유로 날지 못한다.

She cannot fly for an unknown reason.

핑 Ping
숲에 사는 너구리 A racoon living in the forest

손으로 이것저것 만드는 것을 좋아한다. 그렇지만 잘 만드는 것은 아니다. 핑이의 만능 도구 가방에는 도구들 대신 먹을 것이 가득 차 있지 않을까?

He likes to make this and that with his hands. However, he is not necessarily good at it. It is assumed that his fix-it-all tool bag is filled with things to eat instead of tools.

담비 Dambi
보물 수집가 A treasure collector

이곳저곳 돌아다니면서 보물을 찾아, 자신의 창고에 모아 놓는다. 친구들은 그 보물들을 쓰레기라고 하지만, 이번에는 아주 대단한 것을 찾았다고 한다. 어떤 보물일까?

She wanders from place to place to find "treasures" and gathers them in her storage. Her friends call them "trash," but she said she found something really great this time. What will it be?

주머니에 깃털이 있는 옷을 입은 남자
The Man with a Feather in His Pocket
딱 봐도 나쁜 사람 Obviously a bad person

도시의 하얀 탑에서 앵무 로봇을 만들어 사람들한테 나눠 준다. 똑똑한 앵무 로봇은 길도 알려 주고 모르는 것도 알려 준다. 그리고 무료다. 그런데 왜 나쁘지? 음... 뭔가 비밀이 있지 않을까?

He makes parrot robots at the white tower in the city and hands them out to the people. Smart parrot robots let.people know directions and things they do not know themselves. And they are free of charge. So why is he bad? Um… is there some sort of secret?

Chapter 1
앵무 로봇 The Robot Parrots

며칠 전 삽살이가 사는 동네의 모든 집으로 상자가 배달되었어요.
상자 안에는 앵무새처럼 생긴 로봇들이 들어 있었어요.
앵무새처럼 말도 하고, 앵무새처럼 날기도 했어요.

A few days ago, a box was delivered to each and every house in Sapsal's neighborhood.
Inside the boxes were robots that looked like parrots.
They spoke just like parrots do, and they also flew like parrots.

앵무 로봇들은 상자에서 나오자마자 사람들한테 무엇을 먹어야 하는지, 무엇을
입어야 하는지, 어디로 가야 하는지를 말하기 시작했어요.

"제가 하라고 하는 것만 하시면 됩니다. 오늘은 줄무늬 옷을 입으세요."

"오늘은 햄버거를 먹는 날입니다."

"오늘은 김치찌개를 먹는 날이에요."

"이제부터 아무 생각도 할 필요 없어요. 제가 시키는 것을 그대로 하시면 됩니다."

사람들은 잠을 잘 때도, 밖에 나갈 때도, 화장실에 갈 때도, 항상 앵무 로봇을 옆에
두기 시작했어요.

As soon as they came out of the boxes, the robot parrots started telling people what they should eat, what they should wear, and where they should go.

"You just have to do what I tell you to do: Wear striped clothes today."

"Today, you are eating hamburgers."

"Today, you are eating kimchi stew."

"From now on, you don't have to think about anything. You just have to do exactly what I tell you to do."

People started always keeping the robot parrots by their side — when they went to bed, when they went outside, and even when they went to the bathroom.

사람들이 앵무 로봇에 익숙해졌을 때, 앵무 로봇은 사람들한테 어떤
다른 도시에 대해서 말하기 시작했어요.

앵무 로봇은 그 도시에서는 모두가 걱정 없이 편하게 살 수 있다고
말했어요.

그리고 사람들은 하나둘씩 그 도시를 향해 떠나기 시작했어요.

'왜 모두 저 앵무 로봇의 말만 들을까?'

By the time people got used to them, the robot parrots started telling people
about a certain other city.

The robot parrots said that everybody can live comfortably without worries
in that city.

And one by one, people started leaving for the city.

"Why is everyone just listening to the robot parrots?"

삽살이의 가족도 앵무 로봇을 따라 그 도시로 떠났어요.

'어? 그런데 진이는 어디 있지?'

Sapsal's family also followed their robot parrots and left for the city.

"Huh? By the way, where is Jin?"

'어? 집에도 없네?'
아무 말도 없이 갑자기 진이가 사라졌어요.
'진아, 어디 있어?'

"Huh? He's not in the house either."
Jin suddenly disappeared without a word.
"Jin! Where are you?"

삽살이는 지나가는 사람들한테 물었어요.
"저기요, 혹시 파란색 진돗개 보셨어요?"
"저기요? 저기요!"

사람들은 대답이 없었어요.

Sapsal asked people who were passing by.

"Excuse me, have you seen a blue Jindo dog by any chance?"

"Hello? Excuse me?"

People didn't answer.

'저 사람들을 따라가면 진이를 찾을 수 있을까?'

삽살이는 사람들을 따라갔어요.
그리고 오랫동안 달려서 도시의 입구에 도착했어요.

"If I follow these people, can I find Jin?"

Sapsal followed the people.
And after running for a long time, he arrived at the entrance of the city.

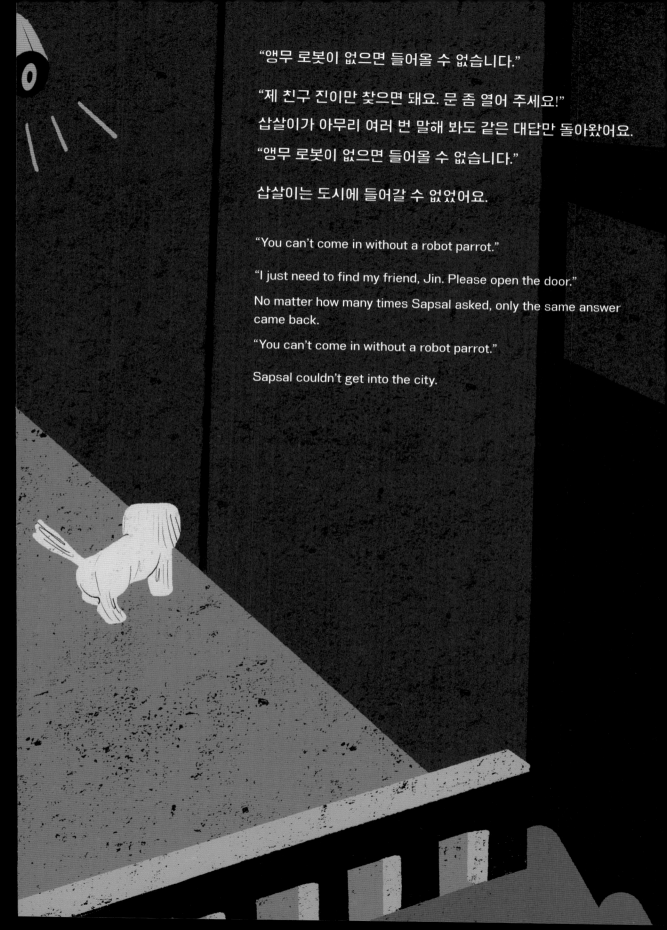

"앵무 로봇이 없으면 들어올 수 없습니다."

"제 친구 진이만 찾으면 돼요. 문 좀 열어 주세요!"
삽살이가 아무리 여러 번 말해 봐도 같은 대답만 돌아왔어요.

"앵무 로봇이 없으면 들어올 수 없습니다."

삽살이는 도시에 들어갈 수 없었어요.

"You can't come in without a robot parrot."

"I just need to find my friend, Jin. Please open the door."
No matter how many times Sapsal asked, only the same answer
came back.

"You can't come in without a robot parrot."

Sapsal couldn't get into the city.

동네를 떠난 사람들은 새 도시에 도착했어요.

이 도시는 조용한 곳이었어요.

사람들의 말소리는 들리지 않고, 앵무 로봇의 말소리만 들렸어요.

The people who left the neighborhood arrived in the new city.

The city was a quiet place.

There were no sounds of people talking, but only sounds of the robot parrots talking.

Chapter 2
하얀 탑 The White Tower

차에서 나온 아이가 뛰어가다가 넘어졌어요.

아이는 넘어지면서 앵무 로봇을 놓쳐서 바닥에 떨어뜨렸어요.

그런데 바닥에 떨어진 앵무 로봇의 입에서 작은 전자 칩이 나왔어요.

전자 칩이 없어진 앵무새는 하늘 높이 날아갔어요.

A child came out from a car and started running, and then he fell down.

As he fell, the child dropped his robot parrot on the ground.

Then a small electronic chip came out from the mouth of the robot parrot that fell to the ground.

After it lost its electronic chip, the parrot flew high into the sky.

"앵무 로봇을 잃어버린 사람은 하얀 탑으로 와서 새로운 오리 로봇을 받아 가세요."

어디에선가 안내 방송이 나왔어요.
아이는 앵무 로봇보다 훨씬 더 크고, 목소리도 훨씬 더 큰 오리 로봇을 받았어요.

"Those who have lost their robot parrot can come to the white tower and get a new robot duck."

An announcement came from somewhere.
The child received a robot duck, which was much bigger and had a much louder voice.

아이가 큰 오리 로봇을 가지고 가는 것을
본 사람들은, 자신의 앵무 로봇을 버리고
하얀 탑으로 걸어갔어요.

그리고 새로운 오리 로봇을 받아서 집으로
돌아갔어요.

When people saw the child carrying his big
robot duck, they threw away their robot
parrots and walked toward the white tower.

Then they received new robot ducks and went
back home.

바로 이 하얀 탑이 동물 로봇을
만드는 곳이었어요.

That white tower was the very place where they made
the animal robots.

하얀 탑의 제일 높은 방 안에는 잡혀 온 새들이 가득했어요.

"여기가 어디지?"
"잠이 들었다가 깨어 보니까 여기네…"
"나는 호수에서 물 마시다가 잡혀 왔어."
"나는 누군가가 던진 빵을 먹다가 잡혔어."

세상 모든 새들이 다 여기에 잡혀 온 것 같았어요.

"쉿, 조용히 해! 온다!"

The topmost room of the white tower was full of birds that had been captured and brought in.

"Where am I?"
"I fell asleep then woke up here…"
"I was drinking water at the lake, then I was brought here."
"I was eating some bread someone threw, then I got caught."

It looked like all the birds in the world had been caught and brought there.

"Shh… Be quiet! He's coming!"

큰 철문이 열리고, 주머니에 깃털이 있는 옷을 입은 남자가 들어왔어요.

"그래, 지금은 실컷 떠들어. 나중에는 내가 하는 말만 그대로 따라 해야 될 거니까."

남자는 새들을 지나서 방 가운데에 있는 테이블로 갔어요. 테이블 위에는 진돗개 한 마리가 누워 있었어요. 진이였어요.

남자는 진이의 머리에 어떤 기계를 붙였어요.

The big steel door opened, and a man wearing clothes with a feather in his pocket came in.

"Fine, talk all you want right now. Later, you'll have to repeat exactly what I tell you."

The man walked past the birds and went to the table that was in the center of the room. On the table laid a Jindo dog. It was Jin.

The man attached a machine to Jin's head.

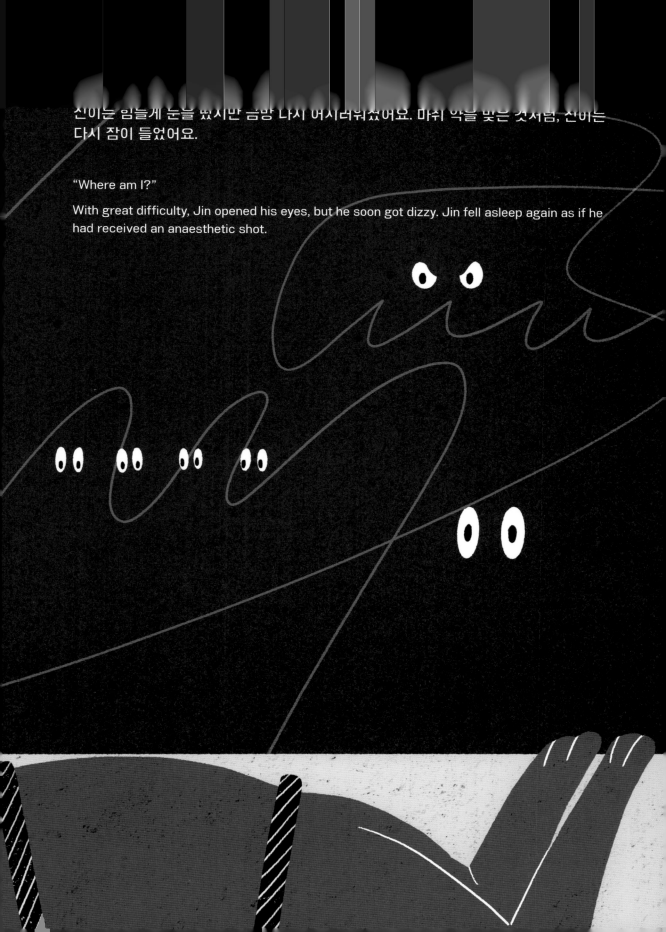

신이는 힘들게 눈을 떴지만 금방 나시 어지러워졌어요. 마취 약을 맞은 것처럼, 신이는 다시 잠이 들었어요.

"Where am I?"

With great difficulty, Jin opened his eyes, but he soon got dizzy. Jin fell asleep again as if he had received an anaesthetic shot.

Chapter 3
삽살이의 하얀 공 Sapsal's White Ball

'진이한테 안 좋은 일이 생긴 것은 아닐까?'
걱정을 하다가 잠이 든 삽살이는, 이상한 느낌이 들어서 잠에서 깼어요.
고개를 들어 창밖을 보니까, 하얀 공이 하늘에 떠 있었어요.

"Perhaps something bad happened to Jin?"
Sapsal, who had fallen asleep while worrying, woke up with a strange sensation.
When he lifted his head and looked out the window, there was a white ball floating in the sky.

"저게 뭐지?"
삽살이가 가까이 가니까, 하늘에 떠 있는 하얀 공은 뒤로 물러났어요.
삽살이가 더 가까이 가니까, 하얀 공은 더 뒤로 물러났어요.
하얀 공은 산과 언덕을 지나 옥수수밭으로 들어갔어요.

"What's that?"
When Sapsal went close, the white ball floating in the sky moved backward.
When Sapsal went closer, the white ball moved farther back.
The white ball passed a mountain and a hill and went into a cornfield.

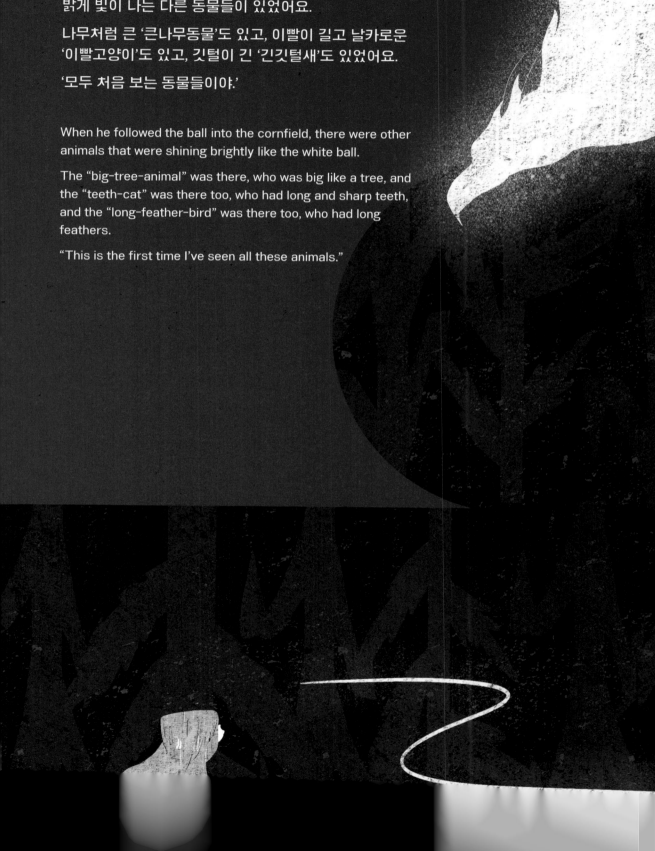

공을 따라 옥수수밭으로 들어가니까, 그곳에는 하얀 공처럼
밝게 빛이 나는 다른 동물들이 있었어요.

나무처럼 큰 '큰나무동물'도 있고, 이빨이 길고 날카로운
'이빨고양이'도 있고, 깃털이 긴 '긴깃털새'도 있었어요.

'모두 처음 보는 동물들이야.'

When he followed the ball into the cornfield, there were other
animals that were shining brightly like the white ball.

The "big-tree-animal" was there, who was big like a tree, and
the "teeth-cat" was there too, who had long and sharp teeth,
and the "long-feather-bird" was there too, who had long
feathers.

"This is the first time I've seen all these animals."

이빨고양이는 하얀 공을 쳐서 삽살이 앞으로 보냈어요.

'나한테 공을 보낸 거지?'

삽살이는 하얀 공을 이빨고양이한테 다시 보냈어요.
이번에는 긴깃털새가 날개로 공을 저 멀리 던졌어요.

'이번에도 나한테 가져오라고 하는 거지?'

The teeth-cat hit the white ball and sent it toward Sapsal.

"Did he send the ball to me?"

Sapsal sent the white ball back to the teeth-cat.
This time, the long-feather-bird threw the ball far
away with its wings.

"I guess they're asking me to fetch it again
this time?"

삽살이는 하얀 동물들과 그렇게 한참을 재미있게 놀았어요.

그러다가 큰나무동물이 실수로 공을 너무 세게 쳐서, 공이 옥수수밭
밖으로 나갔어요.

삽살이가 옥수수밭 밖으로 나가서 하얀 공을 찾아 돌아오니까, 하얀
동물들이 모두 사라지고 없었어요.

Sapsal played with the white animals like that for quite a while.

But then the big-tree-animal hit the ball too hard by mistake, and the ball went
out of the cornfield.

When Sapsal left the cornfield and returned with the white ball, all the white
animals were gone.

다음 날 아침이 되었어요.

"무슨 말이야? 꿈 꾼 거 아니야?"
삽살이가 핑이랑 담비한테 하얀 동물들을 만난 이야기를
해 주었지만, 둘은 삽살이의 이야기를 믿지 않았어요.

"나랑 같이 가 보자. 직접 보여 줄게."

The next morning came around.

"What are you talking about? It was a dream, wasn't it?"

Sapsal told Ping and Dambi about the white animals he met,
but the two didn't believe Sapsal's story.

"Come with me. I'll show them to you myself."

"저기 있다! 하얀 공."
삽살이는 옥수수밭 가운데에 있는 하얀 것을 가리켰어요.

핑이와 담버는 깜짝 놀라 말했어요.
"삽살아, 너 왜 그래?"
"이건 공이 아니잖아..."

삽살이가 하얀 공이라고 한 것은 사실 작은 동물의 머리 뼈였어요.
"땅속에서 나왔나 봐. 다시 넣어 놓자."

"There it is! The white ball."

Sapsal pointed at the white object that was in the middle of the cornfield.

Ping and Dambi were surprised and said,

"Sapsal, what's wrong with you?"

"This isn't a ball…"

What Sapsal called a ball was actually a small animal's skull.

"I guess it came out of the ground. Let's put it back in."

하얀 머리 뼈를 다시 넣으려고 땅을 파다가, 핑이가
뭔가를 봤어요.

"얘들아, 여기에 동물 뼈가 진짜 많아."
핑이가 가리킨 곳에는 삽살이가 어젯밤에 본 동물들의
뼈가 있었어요.

"삽살아... 너 귀신을 보나 봐."

While digging up the ground to put the white skull
back in, Ping saw something.

"Guys, there are a lot of animal bones here."
Where Ping pointed, there were the bones of the
animals that Sapsal saw the previous night.

"Sapsal, I think you can see ghosts."

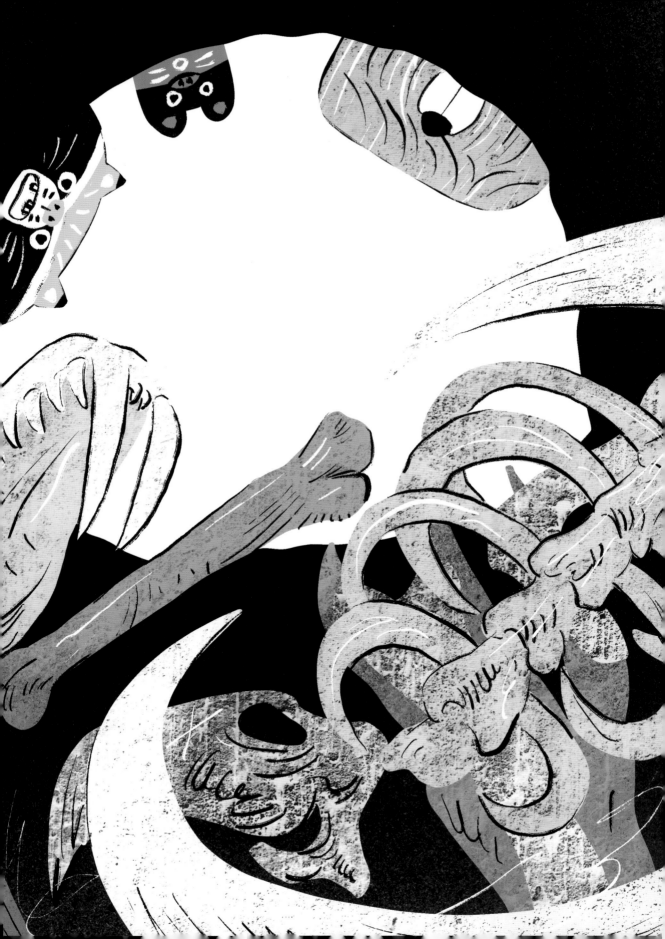

Chapter 4
핑이의 우주선 Ping's Spaceship

"이건 뭐지?"

핑이와 담비 앞에 갑자기 큰 물건이 나타났어요. 핑이와 담비는
이게 무슨 물건인지 궁금했어요.

"이런 물건은 처음 봐. 이거 집 아닐까?"

"집은 아닌 것 같아. 너무 작잖아."

"그래. 너무 작네."

"What's this?"

Suddenly, a large object appeared in front of Ping and Dambi. Ping and Dambi were curious what the object was.

"I've never seen an object like this. Maybe it's a house?"

"I don't think it's a house. It's too small."

"Right. It's too small."

"이거 봐! 여기 문이 있어!"
"정말? 문이 있어? 그럼 자동차 아닐까?"
"바퀴가 없으니까 자동차는 아닌 것 같고..."
"그럼 혹시 외계에서 온 우주선 아닐까?"

"Look! Here's a door!"

"Really? There's a door? Then maybe it's a car?"

"It doesn't have wheels, so I don't think it's a car..."

"Then perhaps it's a spaceship from outer space?"

"우주선?"

둘은 동시에 큰 소리로 말했어요.

"그래! 우주선인 것 같아! 그런데 우주선이 왜 여기 있지? 고장 난 걸까? 나한테 만능 도구 가방이 있으니까, 한번 고쳐 볼게."

핑이는 만능 도구 가방을 가지고 우주선 안으로 들어갔어요.

"A spaceship?" the two said out loud at the same time.

"Yes! I think it's a spaceship! But why is a spaceship here? Is it broken? I have my fix-it-all tool bag, so I'll try fixing it."

Ping went into the spaceship with his fix-it-all tool bag.

핑이는 우주선 안에서 이것저것 살펴보고 있었어요.
그때 갑자기 우주선이 움직였어요.

덜컹덜컹

"으쌰"

쾅

핑이는 밖을 봤어요.

Ping was looking at this and that in the spaceship.
Then suddenly, the spaceship moved.

Rattle rattle.

"Oof!"

THUD.

Ping looked outside.

으쌰

'뭐야? 우주선이 날고 있어!
이거 꿈 아니지?'

"What? The spaceship is flying?
This isn't a dream, is it?"

우주선은 아주 빠른 속도로 어딘가로 날아가고 있었어요.

핑이는 조금씩 겁이 나기 시작했지만, 우주선에서 어떻게 나가는지를 몰랐어요.

'어? 우주선이 멈췄다!'

핑이가 잠시 안심하는 순간, 갑자기 우주선이 쿵 하는 소리를 내면서 아래로 떨어지기 시작했어요.

The spaceship was flying somewhere at a very fast speed.

Ping started getting a little scared, but he didn't know how to get out of the spaceship.

"Huh? The spaceship stopped!"

The moment Ping felt relieved, the spaceship suddenly started falling down with a big thud.

우주선은 데굴데굴 여러 번 굴렀어요. 쿵 하는 소리가
여러 번 들렸어요.

핑이가 창밖을 보니까, 우주선이 호수 속으로 들어가고
있었어요.

The spaceship rolled over several times. There were
several loud thuds.

When Ping looked out the window, the spaceship was going
into a lake.

'여기 있으면 안 돼! 어떻게 나가지?'
핑이는 빨리 우주선의 문을 열어야 했어요.

'문을 어떻게 열지? 아! 이거다!'

다행히 우주선의 문이 열렸고, 핑이는 안전하게
호수 밖으로 나올 수 있었어요.

"I shouldn't stay in here! How do I get out?"
Ping had to open the door of the spaceship quickly.

"How do I open the door? Ah! This is it!"

Luckily, the door of the spaceship opened, and Ping
was able to safely get out of the lake.

Chapter 5
담비의 보물 창고 Dambi's Treasure Storage

담비는 보물을 모으는 취미가 있었어요. 솔방울, 나뭇잎,
사람들이 잃어버린 동전 같은 것들이 담비의 보물이었어요.

그날도 담비는 보물을 찾기 위해 나갔어요. 그리고 담비는
어떤 붉은 나무 위에 걸린 노란색 물건을 봤어요.

'저게 뭐지?'

Dambi had a habit of collecting treasures. Things like pine cones, tree leaves, and coins people have lost were Dambi's treasures.

That day, as usual, Dambi went outside to look for treasures. And she saw a yellow object hanging on this red tree.

"What's that?"

'책? 책이 왜 여기에 있지?'
책은 이 근처에서 쉽게 볼 수 있는 물건이
아니어서 담비는 신났어요.

"A book? Why is a book here?"
A book was not an easy object to see around there,
so Dambi was excited.

"나 보물 찾았어!"

담비는 핑이랑 삽살이한테 가서 자랑했어요. 얼른 책을
보여 주고 싶었어요.

"보물? 또 쓰레기 주운 거 아니야?"

"아니야. 이번에는 너희들이 보면 진짜 깜짝 놀랄 거야."

담비는 둘을 자신의 보물 창고로 데려갔어요.

"I found a treasure!"

Dambi went to Ping and Sapsal and bragged about it. She couldn't
wait to show them the book.

"A treasure? Not another piece of trash you picked up?"

"No. This time, you guys will be really surprised when you see this."

Dambi took the two to her treasure storage.

담비의 보물 창고는 거의 쓰레기장 같았어요. 사람들이 버린 장난감들, 길에서 주운 나뭇잎과 물고기 뼈처럼, 대단하지 않은 물건들이 대부분이었어요.

"저기 있다! 오늘 찾은 노란 책."

Dambi's treasure storage was almost like a dumping ground. There were mostly unremarkable items, like toys people had thrown away and tree leaves and fish bones she had picked up off the street.

"There it is! The yellow book I found today."

담비가 친구들한테 책을 보여 주려고 가까이 가는 순간, 갑자기 책이 움직이기 시작했어요!

꽥!

그리고 갑자기 책이 펴지면서 가운데에서 오리 머리가 나왔어요.

"이게 뭐야?!"

셋은 너무 놀라서 뒤로 넘어질 뻔했어요.

The moment Dambi went closer to the book in order to show it to her friends, the book suddenly started moving.

Quack!

And suddenly, the book opened, and from the middle, a duck's head came out.

"What's this?"

The three were so surprised that they almost fell over backwards.

"이게 무슨 일이야?"

"어떻게 몸은 책이고 얼굴은 오리야?"

오리는 책을 날개처럼 펄럭펄럭 움직였어요.

"What's happening?"

"How is the body a book and the face a duck?"

The duck flapped her book-like wings.

책의 몸을 가진 오리는 반쯤 눈을 떴다가 다시 잠에 빠졌어요.

"이상하다... 이상해."
핑이는 긴장된 표정으로 살금살금 책오리 곁으로 걸어갔어요.

The duck with the book-shaped body opened her eyes about halfway
and then fell asleep again.

"It's strange... It's strange."
Ping snuck up closer to the book-duck with a nervous look on his face.

"죽었어?"
겁이 난 담비는 삽살이 뒤에 숨었어요.

"아니야. 그냥 잠이 든 것 같아."
핑이가 책오리를 살펴보고 말했어요.
"여기에 제목이 있어. 「앵무 로봇」... 책 제목이 「앵무 로봇」이야."

"Is it dead?"
Scared, Dambi hid behind Sapsal.

"No, I think it just fell asleep,"
Ping said, looking at the book-duck.
"Here's the title. *Parrot Robot*. The title of the book is *Parrot Robot*."

Chapter 6
책 읽던 오리
The Duck Who Was Reading a Book

책오리는 원래 계절에 따라 북쪽과 남쪽을 왔다 갔다 하는 철새였어요.

계절이 바뀌고 철새들이 다시 돌아왔을 때, 그 도시는 이제 새들이 쉴 수 있는 곳이 아니었어요.

물고기와 숲 대신에 큰 건물들이 가득했고, 한가운데에는 하얀 탑이 서 있었어요.

The book-duck was originally a migratory bird who traveled between the north and south according to the season.

When the migratory birds came back to the city after the season had changed, the city was not a place where birds could live anymore.

Instead of fish and forests, it was full of big buildings, and in the center, there stood a white tower.

철새들은 하얀 탑 안에 뭐가 있는지 보고 깜짝 놀랐어요.

탑 안은 새장으로 가득했고, 새장에는 많은 새들이 있었어요.

The migratory birds were surprised to see what was in the white tower.

The tower was full of bird cages, and in the cages, there were many birds.

그리고 가운데에 있는 테이블 위에는 파란색 진돗개가 머리에
이상한 것을 쓰고 누워 있었어요.

철새들은 조심히 탑 안으로 들어가서 진돗개 주변을 살펴봤어요.

그 주변에는 여러 가지 기계들과 책 몇 권이 보였어요.

"「앵무 로봇」?"

"「경비 로봇」?"

"이상한 책들이네."

And on the table in the center, a blue Jindo dog was lying down with a strange object
on his head.

The migratory birds carefully went into the tower and looked around the Jindo dog.

Nearby, they could see various types of machines and a few books.

"*Parrot Robot*?"

"*Security Robot*?"

"These are strange books."

"아니, 어떻게 나왔지?"
바로 그때 누군가 큰 소리로 말하면서 새들 주변으로 큰 그물을 던졌어요.

"어서 도망가자!"
다른 새들은 그물에 잡혔지만, 책을 읽고 있던 오리 한 마리만 다행히
그물에 잡히지 않았어요.

"What? How did they get out?" someone said in a loud voice at that moment,
while throwing a large net around the birds.

"Quick! Let's run away!"
The other birds were caught in the net, but just one duck, who had been
reading a book, luckily didn't get caught.

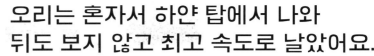

오리는 혼자서 하얀 탑에서 나와
뒤도 보지 않고 최고 속도로 날았어요.

The duck got out of the white tower by herself and, without
even looking back, flew off at the fastest speed.

탑에서 충분히 멀리 왔다고 생각했을 때, 오리는
앞에 보이는 나무 속에 숨었어요.

'여기서 조금만 기다리다가 밤이 되면 다시 돌아가서
모두를 구하자.'

하지만 먼 길을 날아서 온 오리는 너무 피곤해서
깜빡 잠이 들었어요.

When she thought she had come far enough from the
tower, the duck hid herself in a tree that she had seen in
front of her.

"I'm going to wait here for a little bit, and when night
falls, I'm going to go back and save everybody."

But the duck, having flown a long way, felt so tired that
she fell asleep.

"...그리고 몇 시간 뒤에 눈을 뜨니까 봄이 이렇게 색드로 면애 있었어.
책오리는 긴 이야기를 마쳤어요.

"잠깐, 탑 안에 파란색 개가 있다고 하지 않았어?"
삽살이가 깜짝 놀라서 말했어요.

"응, 맞아. 그 안에 새들 말고는 파란색 진돗개 한 마리밖에 없었어."

"진이다!"

"...and when I woke up several hours later, my body had turned into a book like this."
The book-duck finished her long story.

"Wait, didn't you say that there was a blue dog in the tower?"
Sapsal said, surprised.

"Yes, that's right. There are birds in there, but other than them, there is just one other animal, which is a blue Jindo dog."

"That's Jin!"

"진이랑 새들은 하얀 탑으로 잡혀 간 거야!"
삽살이와 핑이는 큰 소리로 말했어요.

"당장 가서 모두를 구하자! 핑이 원정대가 간다!"
"뭐야, 담비 원정대라고 하자."
"삽살이 원정대가 더 좋지 않아?"
"완전 이상해!"
"우리는 진이를 구해야 하니까, 진이 원정대라고 부르자."

"좋아. 진이 원정대가 간다!"

"Jin and the birds were taken to the white tower!" said Sapsal and Ping with a loud voice.

"Let's go and save all of them. The Ping Expedition is on its way!"

"What? Let's call it the Dambi Expedition."

"Doesn't the Sapsal Expedition sound better?"

"It sounds really strange."

"We have to save Jin, so let's call it the Jin Expedition."

"Good. Here comes the Jin Expedition!"

Chapter 7
진이 원정대 The Jin Expedition

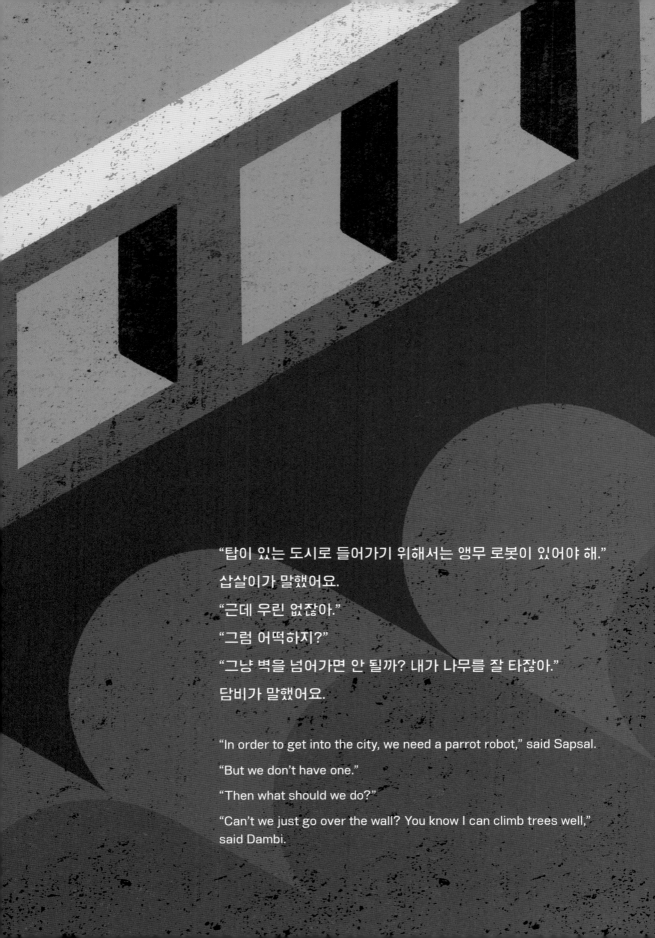

"탑이 있는 도시로 들어가기 위해서는 앵무 로봇이 있어야 해."

삽살이가 말했어요.

"근데 우린 없잖아."

"그럼 어떡하지?"

"그냥 벽을 넘어가면 안 될까? 내가 나무를 잘 타잖아."

담비가 말했어요.

"In order to get into the city, we need a parrot robot," said Sapsal.

"But we don't have one."

"Then what should we do?"

"Can't we just go over the wall? You know I can climb trees well," said Dambi.

"벽이 정말 정말 높아. 그리고 미끄러울 것 같아.
올라가는 게 쉽지 않을 거야."

"그러면 어떻게 하지?"

"The wall is really really high. And I think it'll be slippery.
Climbing up won't be easy."

"Then what should we do?"

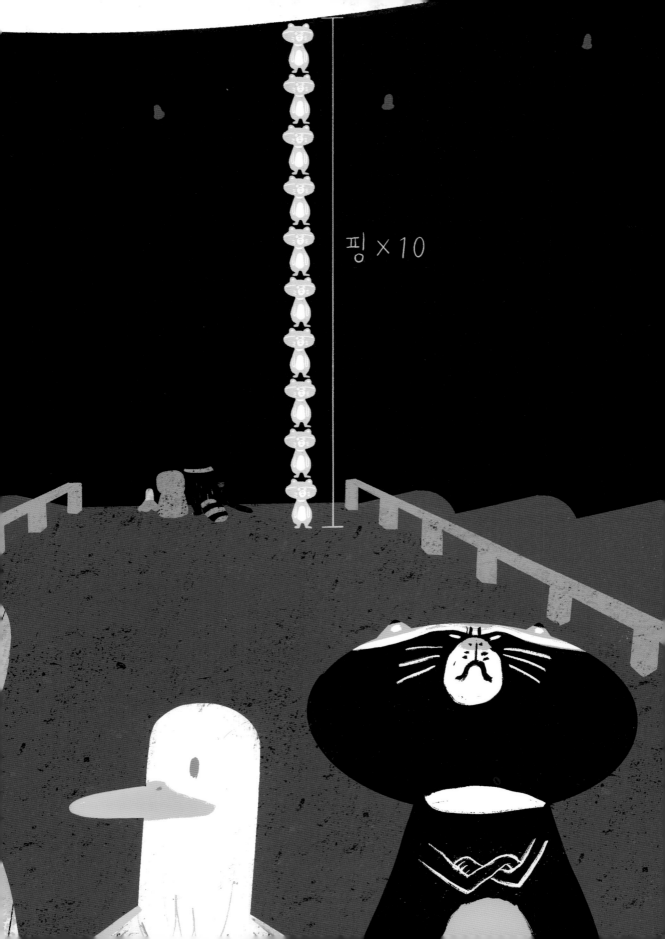

"담비가 큰 나무에 올라가서 벽으로 뛰어 보면 어떨까?"
담비는 큰 나무에 올라가서 벽으로 뛰었어요.
"으악! 너무 멀어."

"그러면 호수에 들어가서 구멍 같은 것을 찾아 보면 어떨까?"
삽살이와 친구들은 호수에 들어갔어요.
"으악! 숨 쉬기 힘들어."

"How about Dambi goes up a big tree and jumps over the wall?"

Dambi climbed a big tree and jumped toward the wall.

"Oh no! It's too far away."

"Then how about we go into the lake and look for something like a hole?"

Sapsal and his friends went into the lake.

"Ahh! I can't breathe."

책오리가 한숨을 쉬면서 말했어요.

"아, 내 몸이 책이 되어서 날 수가 없어. 내가 날 수 있으면 그런 벽은 쉽게 넘을 수 있는데."

"날아? 그래, 맞아! 우주선이 있다는 걸 잊고 있었어!"

"우주선? 지난번 그 우주선? 그거 호수에 빠졌잖아."

"응, 호수에 빠졌지. 그런데 내가 그물로 꺼내서 더 멋지게 바꿨어."

"진짜?"

The book-duck sighed and said, "My body turned into a book, so I can't fly. If I could fly, I could easily go over such a wall."

"Fly? Yes, that's right! I forgot that we have a spaceship!"

"A spaceship? That spaceship from the other day? It fell into the lake."

"Yes, it fell into the lake. But I pulled it out with a net and made it nicer."

"Really?"

"이리 와 봐! 보여 줄게. 나의 첫 우주선, 핑이의 핑퐁호!"

삽살이는 핑이의 우주선을 보고 크게 웃었어요.

"뭐야? 이거... 우주선이 아니고 세탁기잖아."

"세탁기가 뭐야?"

담비는 삽살이의 말이 이해가 안 된다는 표정을 지었어요.

"얘들아, 시간이 없어. 빨리 타자." 핑이가 말했어요.

"Come here! Let me show you. My first spaceship. Ping's Ping Pong Spaceship!"

Sapsal laughed out loud at Ping's spaceship.

"What? This... is not a spaceship. It's a washing machine!"

"What is a washing machine?" Dambi said with a facial expression showing that she didn't understand what Sapsal said.

"Guys, we don't have time. Let's hurry up and get in," said Ping.

"이거 진짜 날 수 있는 거 맞아?"

삽살이는 핑이의 말을 믿을 수 없었어요.

"당연하지. 우주까지는 못 가지만, 저 벽은 쉽게 넘을 수 있어."

핑이가 버튼을 몇 개 누르니까 핑퐁호는 반짝반짝 빛을 내기 시작했어요.

"Are you sure that this thing can really fly?"

Sapsal couldn't believe what Ping said.

"Of course. We can't go to space, but we can go over that wall easily."

Ping pressed a few buttons, and the Ping Pong Spaceship started glowing brightly.

"그럼 출발한다! 모두 꽉 잡아!"
핑이는 큰 소리로 말했어요.

"어디를 잡아야 돼?"
"우리 진짜 하늘로 올라가?"
"출발!"

"Then let's get going! Everybody, hold on tight!"
Ping said in a loud voice.

"What should I hold onto?"
"Are we really going up in the air?"
"Let's go!"

핑퐁호는 시끄러운 소리를 내면서 하늘로 떠올랐어요.

"우와! 날아간다!"

하늘로 떠오른 핑퐁호는 벽을 넘어 도시 안으로 들어갔어요.

The Ping Pong Spaceship flew into the sky with loud sounds.

"Wow! We're flying!"

The Ping Pong Spaceship, high up in the sky, flew over the wall and went into the city.

날아간다

Chapter 8
주머니에 깃털이 있는 옷을 입은 남자
The Man with a Feather in His Pocket

"다들 괜찮지?"

"우주선은 다시 타지 않을 거야."

"어! 저기 하얀 탑이 보인다."

똑같이 생긴 건물들 사이로 하얀 탑이 보였어요.

"Everyone's okay, right?"

"I'm never going to fly in a spaceship again."

"Look! I see the white tower over there."

Between the buildings that all looked the same, they could see a white tower.

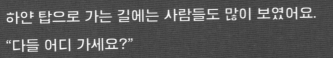

하얀 탑으로 가는 길에는 사람들도 많이 보였어요.

"다들 어디 가세요?"

"몰라. 말 걸지 마. 대답을 하기 위해서는 생각을 해야 되잖아."

진이 원정대는 아무것도 안 하는 사람들을 지나 하얀 탑으로 갔어요.

On their way to the white tower, they also saw many people.

"Where are you all going?

"I don't know. Don't talk to me. To answer you, I'd have to think."

The Jin Expedition went past the people who were not doing anything and went to the white tower.

"내가 먼저 올라가서 줄을 내려 줄게."

담비는 나무 타기 실력을 이용해서 탑의 높은 곳까지 올라갔어요. 그리고 핑이와 삽살이를 위해서 줄을 내려 줬어요.

"빨리 올라와. 조심해! 어, 저기 트럭이 나간다!"

발밑을 보니까 하얀 트럭이 무언가를 가득 싣고 밖으로 나오고 있었어요.

"I will go up first and lower the rope."

Dambi, using her tree-climbing skills, went up to a high part of the tower. Then she lowered a rope for Ping and Sapsal.

"Hurry up and come up. Be careful! Look! There's a truck leaving over there."

Underneath their feet, they saw a white truck coming outside with a full load of something.

"아무도 없는 것 같지?"

"내가 지난번에 왔을 때보다 새들이 많이 사라졌네. 아까 그 트럭에 실려 갔나 봐."

"진이는 아직 여기 있을까?"

"우선 진이를 찾은 다음에, 아직 남아 있는 새들이 있으면 그 새들도 구하자."

그런데 바로 그때, 으르렁 소리가 들렸어요.

"Looks like there's no one here, right?"

"Many of the birds are gone compared to the last time I came here. I guess they were carried away on the truck."

"I wonder if Jin's still here."

"First, we find Jin, then if there are still birds remaining here, let's save the birds, too."

But right at that moment, they heard a roar.

방 안에 빨간 불이 들어오고 경비 로봇이 나타났어요. 경비 로봇은
진이 원정대를 보면서 으르렁 소리를 냈어요.

"어? 저거 진이 아니야?"

"진아, 나야, 삽살이. 너를 구하려고 왔어!"

하지만 머리에 기계를 쓰고 있는 진이는 삽살이를 전혀 알아보지
못하고 큰 소리로 짖었어요.

"진아, 왜 그래?"

"우리를 못 알아보는 것 같아."

A red light came on in the room, and a security robot appeared.
The security robot growled at the Jin Expedition.

"Huh? Isn't that Jin?"

"Jin! It's me, Sapsal! I'm here to save you!"

But Jin, who was wearing a machine on his head, didn't recognize
Sapsal at all and barked loudly.

"Jin, what's wrong?"

"I don't think he recognizes us."

바로 그때 어디선가 큰 그물이 나왔어요. 그리고 진이 뒤에서
주머니에 깃털이 있는 옷을 입은 남자가 나타났어요.

"아니, 넌 그 책 도둑이잖아! 스스로 여기에 다시 돌아왔어? 잘됐다."
그 남자는 앵무 로봇과 목소리가 똑같았어요.

그때 핑이의 만능 도구 가방 속에서 하얀 공이 또르르 나왔어요.
삽살이가 며칠 전에 본 그 머리 뼈였어요.

'어? 머리 뼈잖아.'

Right at that moment, a large net came out, and the man with a feather in his pocket
came out from behind Jin.

"Wait, you're that book thief! You came back here yourself? That's great!"
The man had the same voice as the parrot robots.

Just then, a white ball came rolling out from Ping's fix-it-all tool bag. It was that skull
that Sapsal saw a few days before.

"Huh? It's the skull."

삽살이가 조심히 머리 뼈를 집어 든 순간,
갑자기 하얀 머리 뼈에서 빛이 나기 시작했어요.

The moment Sapsal carefully picked up the skull,
the white skull suddenly started glowing.

그리고 그날 밤에 삽살이가 본
빛나는 동물들이 나타났어요.

으르렁!

이빨고양이는 그물을 끊었어요.

뿌우우!

큰나무동물은 기계들과 새장 문을 부쉈어요.

"아니, 이것들은 다 뭐야?!"

까아악!

긴깃털새는 발로 남자를 잡아 올려서 창문
밖으로 날아갔어요.

"아아악!! 나 좀 내려놔!"

Then the glowing animals that Sapsal saw the other night appeared.

Roar!

The teeth-cat cut the net.

Brrrrrt!

The big-tree-animals broke the machines and bird cages.

"Wait, what are all these things?"

Gasp!

The long-feather-bird picked up the man by the feet and flew out the window.

"Ahh! Put me down!"

하얀 탑 안의 기계들이 깨지고 고장 나니까 새장 안의 새들이 입에서 작은 칩들을 토했어요. 진이의 머리에서도 기계가 떨어지고, 진이가 원래의 모습으로 돌아왔어요.

"진아! 괜찮아?"

"으응... 근데 여기가 어디야? 무슨 일이 일어난 거야?"

"나중에 얘기해 줄게. 빨리 나가자."

When the machines in the tower were destroyed and broken down, the birds in the cages spit small electronic chips up from their mouths. The machine on Jin's head also fell off, and Jin returned to his original appearance.

"Jin! Are you okay?"

"Yes... But where am I? What happened?"

"We'll tell you later. Let's get out of here quickly."

진이와 친구들은 하얀 탑에서 나와 동네로 향했어요.

"그런데 책오리는 왜 원래 모습으로 돌아오지 않지?"

"어떡하지? 다른 방법을 찾아보자."

"그래도 진이를 안전하게 잘 구해서 다행이야. 그리고 책 날개도 꽤 멋있지 않아?"

책오리도 친구들과 함께 동네로 향했어요.

"여러분, 로봇들은 이제 다 사라졌어요. 이제 로봇 말을 안 들어도 돼요. 모두 집으로 돌아가세요!"

"...."

사람들은 아무 말 없이 움직이지 않고 기다렸어요.

누군가 무엇을 하라고 말해 주기를.

Jin and the expedition team left the white tower and headed to their neighborhood.

"But why is the book-duck not returning to her original state?"

"What should we do? Let's find another way to change her back."

"But I'm glad we saved Jin safely and well. And aren't my book wings quite nice too?"

The book-duck also headed back to the neighborhood with the friends.

"Everyone, the robots are all gone. You don't have to listen to the robots anymore. Everyone, go back home!"

"...."

People just waited there without a word and without moving — for someone to tell them what to do.

Glossary

—

Grammar Points

-(으)ㄴ 것 같다	I think...
-(으)ㄴ 다음에	after V-ing
-(으)ㄴ 후에	after V-ing
-(으)ㄴ/는지	whether or not
-(으)니까	since, because, as
-(으)ㄹ 거예요	future tense
-(으)ㄹ 때	when
-(으)ㄹ 뻔하다	to almost + V
-(으)ㄹ 수 있다	can + V
-(으)ㄹ게요	I will + V
-(으)ㄹ까요?	I wonder...
-(으)라고 하다	to tell someone to do something
-(으)려고	in order to + V
-(으)로	toward
-(으)면	if
-(으)면 되다	to be just supposed to + V, to just have to + V, can just + V
-(으)면 안 되다	you should not
-(으)면서	as, while
-(으)세요	imperative (polite)
-(이)랑	with, and
-고	linking verbs; and
-고 싶다	to want to + V
-고 있다	to be + V-ing
-기	to + V, V-ing
-기 시작하다	to start + V-ing

-기 위해(서)	in order to + V	-아/어/여(서)	by V-ing, in order to + V, to V and (then)
-(으)ㄴ/는가	ending used for expressing one's supposition	-아/어/여야 되다/하다	to have to, should, must + A/V
-나 보다, -(으)ㄴ가 보다	I guess, I assume	-아/어/여지다	to improve, to change, to increase
-네요	verb ending used for expressing one's impression of something or surprise toward something	-에	at
		-에 대해서	about
		-에서	at, from
-는 것	to + V, V-ing	-와/과	with, and
-다가	while + V-ing, in the middle of + V-ing	-을/를 위해서	for
-던	verb ending that marks an action or a state that used to take place in the past	-의	of
		-자	let's + V (casual)
		-자마자	as soon as
-도	too, also	-잖아요	You know, Isn't it...?
-들	suffix for plural	-지 마세요	Don't + V (polite)
-만	only	-지 못하다	cannot + V
-보다	than	-지 않다	to not + A/V
-부터	from	-지?	question ending used when you are asking yourself a question
-(으)시-	honorific suffix		
-씩	each, by	-지만	linking verbs; but
-아/어/여	imperative (casual)	-쯤	about, approximately
-아/어/여 놓다	to leave something in a certain state	-처럼	like, similar to
-아/어/여 보다	to try + V-ing	-한테	to (someone)
-아/어/여 있다	to have been put into a certain state	못	cannot + V
-아/어/여 주다	to do something for someone	안	to not + A/V

Glossary

—

Vocabulary

가까이	close
가다	to go
가득하다	to be full
가리키다	to point
가방	bag
가운데	middle, center
가져오다	to fetch
가족	family
가지	kind, sort, type
가지고 가다	to carry, to bring
가지다	to have
갑자기	suddenly
같다	to be same
같은	same * 같은 is the adjective form of 같다.
같이	with, together
개	the counter for objects
거의	almost
걱정	worries
걱정하다	to worry
건물	building
걸리다	to be hung
걸어가다	to walk
겁	fear
겁이 나다	to get scared
것	thing, stuff
경비	security, guard
곁	side
계절	season

고개	head
고개를 들다	to lift one's head
고양이	cat
고장	breakdown
고장이 나다	to be broken
고치다	to fix
곳	place
공	ball
괜찮다	to be okay
구르다	to roll
구멍	hole
구하다	to save
궁금하다	to be curious
권	the counter for books
귀신	ghost
그	that
그곳	there
그날	the other day
그냥	just
그대로	exactly
그때	then
그래	fine, yes
그러다	to do so
	* 그러다 is short for 그리하다.
그런	such
그런데	by the way
그럼	then
	* 그럼 is short for 그러면.

그렇게	like that
	* 그렇게 is the adverb form of 그렇다.
그리고	and
그물	net
근데	by the way
	* 근데 is short for 그런데.
근처	around, near
금방	soon
기계	machine
기다리다	to wait
긴	long
	* 긴 is the modifying form of 길다.
긴장되다	to be nervous
길	street, way
길다	to be long
김치찌개	kimchi stew
깃털	feather
까아악	gasp
깜짝	with surprise
깨지다	to be destroyed
꺼내다	to pull out
꽉	tight
꽤	quite
꽥	quack
꿈	dream
꿈을 꾸다	to dream
끊다	to cut
나	I
나가다	to go outside

나무	tree	높다	to be tall, to be high
나뭇잎	leaf	높은	tall
나오다	to come out		* 높은 is the modifying form of 높다.
나중에	later	높이	high
나타나다	to appear	누군가	someone
날	day	누르다	to press
날개	wing	눈	eye
날다	to fly	눈을 뜨다	to open one's eyes
날아가다	to fly (and go)	눕다	to lie
날카로운	sharp	느낌	sensation, feeling
	* 날카로운 is the modifying form of 날카롭다.	느낌이 들다	to feel
남다	to remain	다	all, every
남자	man, male	다른	different
남쪽	the south		* 다른 is the modifying form of 다르다.
내	I, my	다시	again
내려놓다	to put down	다음	next
내리다	to lower	다행	luck
너	you	다행히	luckily
너무	too	달리다	to run
너희	you (plural)	당연하다	to be natural
넘다	to jump over	당장	right now
넘어가다	to go over	대단하다	to be remarkable
넘어지다	to fall down	대답	answer
넣다	to put in	대답하다	to answer
노란	yellow	대부분	mostly
	* 노란 is the modifying form of 노랗다.	대신에	instead of
노란색	yellow	더	more
놀다	to play	던지다	to throw
놀라다	to be surprised	덜컹덜컹	rattle rattle

데굴데굴	mimetic word for something big rolling
데려가다	to take (someone)
도구	tool
도둑	thief
도망가다	to run away
도시	city
도착하다	to arrive
돌아가다	to go back
돌아오다	to return
동네	neighborhood
동물	animal
동시에	at the same time
동전	coin
되다	to become, to turn
두다	to keep
둘	two
뒤	back
듣다	to listen
들다(1)	to contain, to consist of
들다(2)	to hold, to lift
들리다	to be heard
들어가다	to get in
들어오다	to come in
따라 하다	to repeat
따라가다	to go after
따르다	to follow
땅속	in the ground
떠나다	to leave
떠들다	to talk, to chat

떠오르다	to float
떨어뜨리다	to drop
떨어지다	to be dropped, to be fell down
또	again
또르르	mimetic word for something small rolling lightly
똑같다	to be the same
똑같이	the same
뛰다	to run, to jump
뛰어가다	to run
뜨다	to float
로봇	robot
마리	the counter for animals
마시다	to drink
마취	anaesthetic
마치다	to finish
만나다	to meet
만능	omnipotent, all-purpose
만드는	making * 만드는 is the adjective form of 만들다.
많다	to be many
많은	a lot of, many * 많은 is the modifying form of 많다.
많이	a lot, many
말	words
말고(는)	other than
말소리	sounds of talking
말을 걸다	to talk to

말하다	to speak	무엇	what
맞다(1)	to be right	문	door
맞다(2)	to receive, to get a shot	묻다	to ask
머리	head	물	water
먹는	eating	물건	object
	* 먹는 is the adjective form of 먹다.	물고기	fish
먹다	to eat	물러나다	to move backward
먼	far	뭐	what
	* 먼 is the modifying form of 멀다.		* 뭐 is short for 무엇
먼저	first	뭔가	something
멀다	to be far		* 뭔가 is short for 무언가
멀리	far away	미끄럽다	to be slippery
멈추다	to stop	믿다	to believe
멋있다	to be nice	바꾸다	to change (something)
멋지게	nicely	바뀌다	to be changed
	* 멋지게 is the adverb form of 멋지다.	바닥	ground
		바로	the very
며칠	a few days	바퀴	wheel
몇	several	밖	outside
모두	all	반	half
모든	all, every	반짝반짝	glowing
모르다	to not know	받다	to get, to receive
모습	appearance	발	foot, feet
모으는	collecting	밝게	brightly
	* 모으는 is the adjective form of 모으다.		* 밝게 is the adverb form of 밝다.
목소리	voice	방	room
몸	body	방법	way, method
무슨	which	방송	broadcasting
무언가	something	배달되다	to be delivered
		버리다	to throw away

버튼	button
벽	wall
변하다	to turn
보내다	to send
보다	to see
보물	treasure
보이다(1)	to be seen
보이다(2)	to show
부수다	to break
북쪽	the north
불	light
붉은	red
	* 붉은 is the modifying form of 붉다.
붙이다	to attach
빛	light, glow
빛을 내다	to glow
빛이 나는	shining
	* 나는 is the modifying form of 나다.
빠른	fast
	* 빠른 is the modifying form of 빠르다.
빠지다	to fall
빨간	red
	* 빨간 is the modifying form of 빨갛다.
빨리	quickly
빵	bread
뼈	bone
뿌우우	brrrrt

사는	live
	* 사는 is the adjective form of 살다.
사라지다	to disappear
사람	person, people
사실	actually
사이	between
산	mountain
살금살금	to sneak
살다	to live
살펴보다	to look at
상자	box
새(1)	new
새(2)	bird
새로운	new
	* 새로운 is the modifying form of 새롭다.
새장	bird cage
생각	thinking, thoughts
생각하다	to think
생기다	to look like
서다	to stand
세게	hard, strongly
	* 세게 is the adverb form of 세다.
세상	world
세탁기	washing machine
셋	three
소리	sound
소리를 내다	to make sound
속	in, inside

속도	speed	아니다	to be not
솔방울	pine cone	아니야	no (casual)
순간	moment	아래	down
숨	breath	아무	any
숨다	to hide	아무것도	nothing
숨을 쉬다	to breathe	아무도	no one
숲	forest	아무리 -아/어/여도	no matter how, even though, even if
쉬다	to take a rest	아이	child
쉽게	easily	아주	very
	* 쉽게 is the adverb form of 쉽다.	아직	still, yet
쉽다	to be easy	아침	morning
쉿	shh	안	in, inside
스스로	by oneself	안내	announcement
시간	time	안심하다	to feel relieved
시간	time	안전하게	safely
시끄러운	noisy		* 안전하게 is the adverb form of 안전하다.
	* 시끄러운 is the modifying form of 시끄럽다.	알아보다	to recognize
시작하다	to start	앞	front
시키다	to order	앵무새	parrot
신이 나다	to be excited = 신나다	약	medicine, shot
싣다	to carry	얘	hey; used a way to call a child among children or by adults. = 야
실력	skill	얘기하다	to tell
실리다	to be carried		* 얘기하다 is short for 이야기하다
실수로	by mistake		
실컷	as much as one wishes	얘들아	hey guys
쓰다	to put on	어디	where
쓰레기	trash	어디에선가	from somewhere
쓰레기장	dumping ground	어딘가	somewhere
아까	a while ago		

어떡하다	to do how	완전	absolutely, completely
	* 어떡하다 is short for 어떻게 하다	왜	why
어떤	certain	외계	space
	* 어떤 is the modifying form of 어떻다.	우리	we
어떻게	how	우선	first
어서	quickly	우와	wow
어젯밤	the previous night	우주	space
어지러워지다	to get dizzy	우주선	spaceship
언덕	hill	움직이다	to move
얼굴	face	웃다	to laugh
얼른	quickly	원래	originally
없다	to not have, to not exist	원정대	expedition
없어지다	to be lost, to disappear	위	up
없이	without	으르렁	roar
여기	here	으쌰	oof
여러 번	a few times	으악	ahh
여러분	everyone	응	yes
열다	to open	이	this
열리다	to be opened	이거 (이것)	this one
옆	side	이것저것	this and that
오늘	today	이런	like this
오다	to come		* 이런 is the modifying form of 이렇다.
오랫동안	for a long time	이렇게	like this
오리	duck	이리	this way, over here
옥수수밭	cornfield	이번	this time
올라가다	to go up, to climb up	이빨	teeth
올라오다	to come up	이상하다	to be strange
올리다	to lift, to raise	이상한	strange
옷	clothes		* 이상한 is the modifying form of 이상하다.

이야기	story		잠	sleep
이야기하다	to tell		잠깐	for a little while, for a moment
이용하다	to use			
이제	now		잠시	for a little while, for a moment
이해	understanding			
이해되다	to understand		잠이 깨다	to wake up
익숙하다	to get used to		잠이 들다	to fall asleep
일	something, event, affair		잡다	to hold, to grab
일어나다	to happen		잡히다	to be caught, to be captured
잃어버리다	to lose			
입	mouth		장난감	toys
입구	entrance		재미있게	fun, playfully
입다	to wear			* 재미있게 is the adverb form of 재미있다.
입은	wearing			
	* 입은 is the adjective form of 입다.		저	that
			저거 (저것)	that one
있는	with, having, existing		저기	there
	* 있는 is the modifying form of 있다.		저기요	excuse me
			전	ago, before
있다	to have, to exist		전	before
잊다	to forget		전자	electronic
자다	to sleep		전혀	at all
자동차	car		정말	really
자랑하다	to brag		제	I
자신	oneself		제목	title
작다	to be small		제일	most
작은	small		조금	a little
	* 작은 is the modifying form of 작다.		조금씩	little by little
			조심하다	to be careful
잘	well		조심히	carefully
잘되다	to be great, to work well			

조용한	quiet
	* 조용한 is the modifying form of 조용하다.
조용히	quietly
좀	please
좋다	to be good
좋은	good
	* 좋은 is the modifying form of 좋다.
주머니	pocket
주변	around
죽다	to die
줄	rope
줄무늬	striped
줍다	to pick up
지금	(right) now
지나가다	to pass by
지나다	to pass by, to walk past
지난번	the other day, last time
직접	oneself, in person
진돗개	Jindo dog
진짜	really
집	house
집다	to pick up
짖다	to bark
차	car
창고	storage
창밖	out the window
찾다	to find
책	book
처음	first

철	steel, iron
철새	migratory bird
첫	first
최고	the best
출발	departure
출발하다	to depart, to leave
충분히	enough
취미	hobby
치다	to hit
친구	friend
칩	chip
쿵	thud
크게	loudly
크다	to be big
큰	big
	* 큰 is the modifying form of 크다.
타기	climbing, riding
탑	tower
테이블	table
토하다	to spit up
트럭	truck
파다	to dig
파란색	blue
펄럭펄럭	flap flap
펴지다	to be opened
편하게	comfortably
	* 편하게 is the adverb form of 편하다.
표정	look, facial expression

표정을 짓다	to make a facial expression
피곤하다	to be tired
필요 없다	to do not have to
하나둘	one or two
하늘	sky
하다	to do
하얀	white
	* 하얀 is the modifying form of 하얗다.
하지만	but, however
한	one
	* 한 is the modifying form of 하나.
한가운데	the very middle
한번	try
한숨	sigh
한참	for quite a while
함께	with together
항상	always
햄버거	hamburger
향하다	to head (for/toward)
호수	lake
혹시	by any chance
혼자(서)	by oneself, alone
화장실	bathroom
훨씬	much
힘들게	with difficulty
	* 힘들게 is the adverb from of 힘들다.
힘들다	to be tired